Homework *for the* Heart

Homework *for the* Heart

Devotions for Teachers

Lisa Flinn &
Barbara Younger

DIMENSIONS
FOR LIVING
NASHVILLE

HOMEWORK FOR THE HEART
DEVOTIONS FOR TEACHERS

This book is printed on acid-free paper.

Library of Congress Cataloging-in-Publication Data

Flinn, Lisa, 1951-
Homework for the heart : devotions for teachers / Lisa Flinn and Barbara Younger.
p. cm.
ISBN 0-687-04589-4 (pbk. : alk. paper)
1. Teachers—Prayer-books and devotions—English. I. Younger, Barbara, 1954- II. Title.
BV4596.T43 F575 2003
242' .68—dc21

2002014385

03 04 05 06 07 08 09 10 11 12—10 9 8 7 6 5 4 3 2 1
MANUFACTURED IN THE UNITED STATES OF AMERICA

To Henrietta Auman and Tommy Leonard,

two teachers who gave from their hearts

Contents

A Word from the Authors 9
1. The Apples of Our Eyes 11
2. Things Visible and Invisible 12
3. The Golden Rule 13
4. A Time to Laugh 14
5. Oh, Those Tests 15
6. Don't Drop That Tray! 16
7. The Weight of the World 18
8. Gathering Lambs 20
9. Mark That Place 22
10. Whistles and Whispers 24
11. The Good Book 26
12. Pomp and Circumstance 28
13. In Plenty and in Need 30
14. A Time for Everything 31
15. Sticks and Stones 32
16. The Way 33
17. Tablets of Human Hearts 34
18. Ralph the Guinea Pig 35
19. The Work of Our Hands 37
20. The Cure 38
21. Share the Faith 40
22. Fire! 42
23. Smile for the Camera 43
24. In Paul's Footsteps 45
25. Wonderful Words 46
26. Settling into Prayer 47

27. Children of Light 49
28. Oh, Those Earthly Treasures 51
29. The Writing on the Wall 53
30. Showing Honor 55
31. Time-Out! 57
32. Lines and Squiggles 58
33. At the Crossroads 60
34. Love Is 61
35. Count Those Days! 63
36. Our Spinning Planet 65
37. Into the Future 67
38. Circle of Believers 68
39. Serendipity! 69
40. A Need for Feedback 70
41. By Our Love 72
42. The Field Is the World 74
43. The Fun Stuff! 76
44. Special Delivery 77
45. Hungry? 79
46. Getting the Picture 81
47. What Counts? 82
48. A Mighty Tall Tower 84
49. Happy Birthday to You 86
50. Building on Solid Rock 88
51. Red Sky 90
52. Gum Day 91

A Word from the Authors

Rulers, staplers, backpacks, books, scissors, dictionaries, lockers, cafeteria trays, globes, computers, guinea pigs—such is the stuff of our schools and classrooms. When Lisa and I began to think about writing this collection of devotions, we came upon the idea of presenting an "object lesson" in a lesson plan format, centering each devotion on an object quite familiar to teachers. Although some of the objects are more common in elementary classrooms, the devotional insights and practical applications we share will speak to teachers of all grade levels and subjects—whether their students are learning how to read or how to solve algebra problems.

Ever since I was a little girl growing up in Baltimore, I have been a collector. I began with dolls and books. I now have all sorts of collections from old toys to bookmarks to hatboxes. As I arrange, organize, or dust each item, I like to think about where it came from, why I find it interesting, and what makes it useful or unique. When I work with children as a Sunday school teacher or a visiting author to schools, I often bring along objects from my collections to share with them. Kids like to think about the objects, too, and their importance to the topic at hand.

In *Homework for the Heart,* we have chosen an object for each devotion, and have connected these objects to both teaching and the Christian faith. We offer you encouragement and our enthusiastic support as you carry on one of the world's most challenging professions. That's *our* object!

Barbara Younger

Do you remember a defining moment that led you to become a teacher? My own heart was opened to the mysteries and miracles of teaching during the summer I taught English as a second language. Having just turned sixteen, I was intrigued with driving through the Indiana countryside to the migrant labor camp. Once there, I worked for hours around a picnic table with truly determined students.

I believe that God guided me to that volunteer experience. Teaching that summer influenced my course of study at college and later, along with degrees and recommendations, secured my first position as a reading specialist.

Throughout the years, I've known God's hand in my life, especially in the blessings that have linked Barbara and me as writing partners. Our work together has fostered a wonderful friendship and helped us along our spiritual paths.

There is a spiritual lesson plan for each of us. As with our students, it's our choice to listen and observe; study and reflect; pray and practice what God teaches us.

Gold stars and all good wishes to you! We hope these devotions will be happy homework for your teaching heart.

Lisa Flinn

1. The Apples of Our Eyes

Object: *Apples*

Theme: *Resting in God's Care*

Textbook Reading: *Psalm 17:8 ~ Keep me as the apple of your eye; hide me in the shadow of your wings.* (NIV)

Lesson: Apples: a timeless symbol of students' love for their teachers. They bring us other gifts, too: a picture for our desk, flowers from the backyard, cookies baked the night before, an interesting rock discovered on the way to school. And we appreciate these gifts as well.

Our students might exhaust us, exasperate us, and infuriate us, but, praise God, we love them. Sometimes we worry about them as if they were our own. Yet we know that they are not our own, which can make the worrying all the more frustrating. When problems that are beyond our abilities to solve arise with students, we can pray for them, knowing that they are in the hands of God.

The next time someone in your class brings you an apple, slice it in half to show your students the star formed by the seeds inside. Or surprise your older kids by bringing them apples. Years ago, folks made wishes on apple stars. Encourage your kids to make their own wishes, and, as they do, say your wish and prayer that God will guard and keep all your students as the apples of God's eye.

Extra Credit: One day this week, when you get home from school, put your feet up, close your eyes, and slowly crunch and relish each and every bite of a delicious, nutritious apple. You deserve it!

A Word with the "Principal": God of the young and the old, in my classroom may your caring spirit embrace both teacher and students. Amen.

2. Things Visible and Invisible

Object: *Microscopes*

Theme: *Having Faith*

Textbook Reading: ***Hebrews 11:1 ~ Now faith is the assurance of things hoped for, the conviction of things not seen.***

Lesson: Thanks to Zacharias Janssen, a Dutch spectacle-maker, students in today's classrooms are able to use one of their favorite scientific instruments. Most historians credit Janssen for coming up with the concept of the compound microscope, a scope with two lenses: an objective lens that magnifies the object, and an ocular lens that then magnifies this image. The development of the microscope led to the birth of the field of microbiology as parts of life never seen before could now be seen.

Yet there are parts of life we still cannot see. We cannot see heaven, and we cannot see God. We can see Jesus, though, through the accounts of his life and his teachings recorded in the Bible. As we read the words that Jesus spoke, he enables us to begin to envision the invisible. Then faith comes in, for faith is indeed "the assurance of things hoped for, the conviction of things not seen."

Pop Quiz: If you could ask Jesus one question that would help you see God's kingdom more clearly, what would it be?

A Word with the "Principal": God of all things visible and invisible, give me the assurance of the things I hope for: your continued love and your promise of eternal life. Amen.

3. The Golden Rule

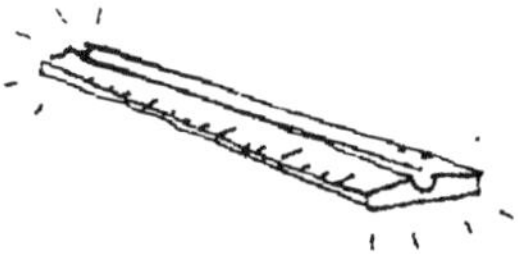

Object: *Rulers*

Theme: *Loving Others*

Textbook Reading: *Luke 6:31 ~ "Do to others as you would have them do to you."* (NIV)

Lesson: Years ago, rulers were sometimes used in classrooms to slap the hands of wayward students. What a sad use for such a useful object. And what a way for teachers to violate the Golden Rule: "Do to others as you would have them do to you."

We have heard over and over again that children learn best by example. But the school day can be a long one, and it's not always easy to continue to be the cheerful, patient, consistent teacher you start out to be each morning. That's when the Golden Rule can help. Jesus, our loving teacher, has set a simple yet clear standard for measuring how we should behave toward others.

Can you remember how it felt to leave your homework at home? Come to school after a fight with your parent or sibling? Be fussed at for something you didn't mean to do? Feel hurt because of a caustic remark? Sure you can!

And that's why, for all teachers, the golden rule is pure gold.

Show and Tell: Kids of all ages enjoy hearing of your childhood adventures and misadventures. Don't hesitate to share with them your school experiences. Why not bring in some of your artwork, spelling tests, essays, and, if you're brave enough, school pictures?

A Word with the "Principal": Loving God, help me to remember to live the Golden Rule as I teach your children. Amen.

4. A Time to Laugh

Object: ***Drinking Fountains***

Theme: ***Knowing the Wisdom of Laughter***

Textbook Reading: ***Proverbs 13:14 ~ The teaching of the wise is a fountain of life.*** **(NIV)**

Lesson: There is a college president who delights students each year by joining them in the annual campus slip and slide. At a college where dedicated teaching is the faculty's first priority, the president sets a wise example. Good teaching and good fun can go hand in hand.

As all teachers know, it's finding the gentle balance between schoolwork and fun that gets tricky. With elementary students, deciding how many trips they can take to the drinking fountain in one day is tricky, too. Young children especially adore drinking fountains. Treks to that favored place often become events of great merriment, particularly if the fountain happens to be the sort that sends a stream of cold water high into the air!

The Bible assures us that there is indeed "a time to laugh" (Ecclesiastes 3:4 NIV). As human beings fashioned in God's image, we can believe that God smiles on our laughter.

When creative teaching, silly situations, or your witty students send your class into gales of laughter, don't rush to make them hush. Wise teachers know that laughter is part of the joyous fountain of life.

Group Work: When your class (even a class of older kids) seems to be in a particularly dour mood, play the "Don't Smile Game." Have them pair up and stare at each other without smiling. Bet they can't do it!

A Word with the "Principal": God of tears and laughter, let me laugh with my students whenever the time is right! Amen.

5. Oh, Those Tests

Object: *Standardized Tests*

Theme: *Seeing All Students as a Marvel of God*

Textbook Reading: ***Galatians 6:4 ~ All must test their own work; then that work, rather than their neighbor's work, will become a cause for pride.***

Lesson: Standardized tests! Say the word around any group of teachers and opinions will fly. Maria Mitchell, the first woman astronomer and a professor at the newly founded Vassar College in the nineteenth century, refused to give grades, saying, "You cannot mark a human mind."* To test or not to test: that will, no doubt, continue to be one of the questions of this century.

Do standardized tests mark the minds of those who don't do well on them, discouraging students and their parents? How do we help a student understand that his or her mind is more than a score on a test?

As we watch the minds of our students develop, may we remember that they are each the work of a loving and brilliant creator, no matter what their test scores. God has graced every human being with amazing qualities beyond measure.

Extra Credit: Go down your class list, reading one name at a time. After each name, think of a talent or personality trait of this student that is noteworthy. Make an effort to mention the attributes you thought of as you work with your kids in the coming weeks.

A Word with the "Principal": God of all, thank you for making each and every one of my students a marvel of your creation. Amen.

---

*Maria Mitchell quoted in *Notable American Women,* Volume II (Harvard University Press, 1972), p. 553.

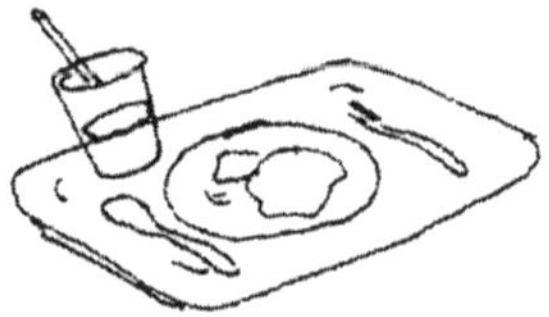

6. Don't Drop That Tray!

Object: *Cafeteria Trays*

Theme: *Experiencing and Sharing God's Care and Encouragement*

Textbook Reading: *Deuteronomy 1:31 ~ And in the wilderness, . . . you saw how the* LORD *your God carried you, just as one carries a child, all the way that you traveled until you reached this place.*

Lesson: The early years of elementary school present many challenges, but for some there is none so daunting as learning to carry the cafeteria tray.

Watch the body language of children as they carry them. Some go barreling through the crowd right to their tables, with no concern about dropping the tray. Others take careful but confident steps until they reach their destination. Still others take baby steps, stopping every few feet and eyeing the items on the tray with worried expressions. And whatever the body language may be, those trays do sometimes land on the floor of the cafeteria.

As teachers, we can't carry the trays for our students, but we can encourage them and help them recover from their spills. Similarly, God can't do our teaching for us, but God can encourage and guide us when we make mistakes.

Now about that cafeteria food . . .

Group Work: With younger kids, play "Tray Relay." Players take turns piling blocks or other items onto a tray and carrying the tray back to the next person in line. For older kids, try "Memory Tray." Arrange items related to a science or social studies unit on a tray. Give the kids thirty seconds to look at the items; then whisk the tray away.

They must do their best to remember and write down the contents of the tray.

A *Word with the* "*Principal*": Encourage me, Lord, as I carry a heavy teaching load, and help me to encourage my students as they carry themselves through school. Amen.

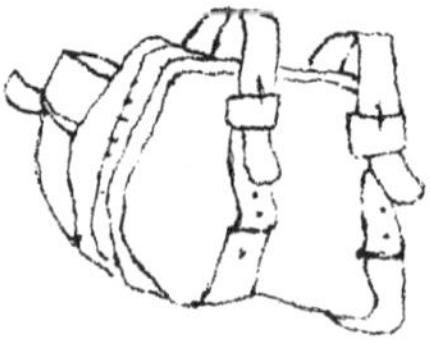

7. The Weight of the World

Object: *Backpacks*

Theme: *Encouraging and Inspiring Students*

Textbook Reading: *Ecclesiastes 12:12 ~ Of making many books there is no end, and much study wearies the body.* **(NIV)**

Lesson: When we pick up a student's backpack, we often can't believe how heavy it is. No wonder kids can seem as if they have the weight of the world on their shoulders: They almost do!

Until textbook publishers develop a way to make their books lighter in weight, there's not much that we can do about heavy backpacks. In elementary schools, we can arrange homework assignments so that kids only need to take home a textbook or two each night; but in high school, this gets more difficult. Some students now use rolling backpacks, but these can be dangerous in crowded hallways. We can only hope that just around the corner there is a solution to the problem of heavy book bags.

And how can we help our students who have heavy hearts from too much studying? We can lighten their burdens by talking to them about how to manage their workloads, by coordinating assignments with other teachers, and by surprising them with breaks from daily routine and nightly homework.

Extra Credit: Occasionally send encouraging messages home in those heavy backpacks. Photocopy quotations, cartoons, or inspiring words and fold them into small squares. Give them to your students at the end of class, with careful instructions that they are not to unfold the message until they open their book bags to do their homework.

A Word with the "Principal": Dear God, please give me the energy and the enthusiasm to light and ignite a spark for learning in the children I teach every day. Amen.

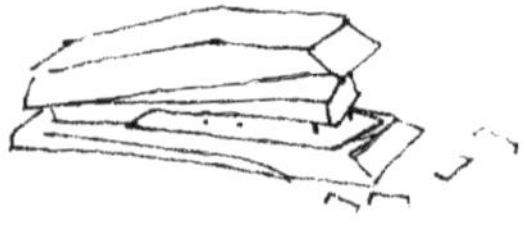

8. Gathering Lambs

Object: *Staplers*

Theme: *Shepherding with Love*

Textbook Reading: *Isaiah 40:11 ~ He will feed his flock like a shepherd; he will gather the lambs in his arms.*

Lesson: Staplers—what a clever way to gather papers together! But staplers tend to wander off. If only we could keep them safe on our desks.

Children—they are clever inventions, too. But, likewise, children tend to wander off. If only we could keep them safe in our classrooms. Kids wander off in all sorts of ways. Sometimes a child literally wanders off, bringing instant panic when we realize he or she is missing. Other times, their wandering is actually dawdling. Perhaps they take a slow journey back from delivering the attendance sheet or some other item to the office, returning by way of the drinking fountain, the media center, or the aquarium in the lobby.

It's when students wander off in spirit—physically present but emotionally drifting—that we are faced with some of our greatest challenges as educators. A concerned word or an encouraging note may be all it takes to bring a student back, but the solution is not always so simple. As you struggle with this dilemma, it can help to keep a picture of Jesus, our shepherd, in your mind. God sent Jesus to gather the lambs. As you work on gathering and keeping your lambs, remember the power of love—your love and the love of God's Son for us all.

Pop Quiz: Which students are you especially concerned

about this week? Why? What can you do to shepherd them in love?

A *Word with the* "Principal": Dear God, as I remember the image of Jesus gathering the lambs, help me to gather my students and keep them safe through the power of your love. Amen.

9. Mark That Place

Object: ***Bookmarks***

Theme: ***Imparting a Love of Reading***

Textbook Reading: ***Nehemiah 8:5 ~ And Ezra opened the book in the sight of all the people, for he was standing above all the people; and when he opened it, all the people stood up.***

Lesson: The people stood up when Ezra opened the book.

How do we get our students to stand up and take notice of the wonderful books in our world today? There is no easy answer, but here are a few ideas:

- Talk about your own reading. Let kids know that you are sleepy this morning because you stayed up too late reading a book by your favorite author!
- Resist being a book snob. Be open to the books your students enjoy reading.
- Introduce them to award-winners, but encourage them to form their own likes and dislikes.
- Assign creative book reports that enable kids to respond to the book—not simply write sentence after sentence.
- Read to your students whether they are four or fourteen. And don't forget the many age-appropriate picture books for older kids.
- Lavish them with bookmarks!
- Emphasize the importance of reading to all subject areas, from science to math to history.

Extra Credit: Use a paper cutter and retired wallpaper from a local paint and decorating store to make no-cost bookmarks. Put them in a basket and let the children choose the ones they like. They will relish the varieties of colors, textures, and designs. Or, for older students, give them colorful or trendy bookmarks.

A *Word with the* "*Principal*": God of all words, books can change lives. I pray that I can encourage my students to become lifelong readers. Amen.

10. Whistles and Whispers

Object: *Whistles*

Theme: *Choosing Words with Care*

Textbook Reading: *Proverbs 4:20 ~ My child, be attentive to my words; incline your ear to my sayings.*

Lesson: There's the whistle!

Why is it that kids almost always respond to the whistle that sounds the beginning of a game or the end of recess; yet when it comes to words, they often close their ears? How can we, as teachers, use words that really "whistle" at students in an upbeat and positive way?

Children of all ages respond to creative language. They like new and unusual words, interesting phrases, inspiring quotations, and engaging stories, riddles, rhymes, and rhythms. They also like familiar language and fun repetition, and they're happy to hear you say your favorite expressions over and over again. And don't forget the longtime teacher's trick: If you really want kids to listen, whisper!

When we pray, we use words. Sometimes we take comfort in the familiar: The repetition of the Lord's Prayer, a beloved grace, or even the bedtime prayer of our childhood. But other times our words are uniquely our own, as we reach out to touch God with words of worry or gratitude or confession. Whether we "whistle" at God with great boldness or whisper in our quietest voice, God responds to our words with love and understanding.

Words to teach and words to pray; may we use them well each day!

Show and Tell: Think of one of your favorite words, one of your favorite expressions, and one of your favorite quotations. Creatively include each of them in your teaching this week. At home, let these beloved words find their way into one of your prayers, too.

A *Word with the* "*Principal*": Holy God, help me to choose words that will encourage the students I teach to listen with attentive and eager ears. Amen.

11. The Good Book

Object: ***Books***

Theme: ***Being Grateful for the Word of God***

Textbook Reading: ***John 1:1 ~ In the beginning was the Word, and the word was with God, and the Word was God.*** **(NIV)**

Lesson:

Books on audiotape
Encyclopedias on CD
E-books on computer screens
What would Gutenberg think?

Gutenberg's invention of a movable type printing press in the mid-1400s brought about the first book to be mass produced, the Latin Bible. His dream was to create liturgical works that were as beautiful and colorful as hand-wrought illuminated manuscripts. Although we cannot know the full intention of his dream, we know one of its outcomes was to make the Holy Word available to more people.

This technological breakthrough naturally led to the publication of books on a variety of subjects. More than five hundred years later, the books in our schools, libraries, and bookstores are a legacy to Gutenberg's vision. As the accessibility of the printed word abounds, so does the freedom to study, exchange ideas, and discuss beliefs.

What would Gutenberg think of the inventions of the information age? He might grieve the loss of artistic elegance in much of our reading matter, but most likely he would champion the abundance of Bibles and other texts offered in a range of formats and languages for a world full of readers.

Extra Credit: Read the eloquent words of the Gospel of John 1:1-23.

A Word with the "Principal": Holy One, I am grateful for the divinely inspired words of the Bible, and for the freedom to read them. Amen.

12. Pomp and Circumstance

Object: *Caps and Gowns*

Theme: *Grooming Lifelong Learners*

Textbook Reading: *Matthew 11:29a ~ Take my yoke upon you and learn from me.* (NIV)

Lesson: If you're an elementary school teacher and you stay in a school system long enough, the day will come when you see your former students march across the stage to receive their diplomas. If you're a middle or high school teacher, the wait won't be as long. Garbed in the customary caps and gowns, they look quite composed and mature. Proud of their achievements and dignified by their regalia, the students seem transformed. As you watch the robes fluttering and the tassels swinging, you may wonder how and when this costume became a tradition.

Eight hundred years ago, robes were common attire in medieval Europe, where tradesmen, professionals, and clerical orders each adopted particular styles. The academics, who organized guilds from Paris to Bologna to Oxford, assumed the clerical dress of robes with cowls, hoods, or skullcaps. By the fourteenth century Cambridge and Oxford Universities insisted on the wearing of long gowns and the approval of all trimmings. Somewhere along the way, cowls and hoods were cut down in size, and caps, such as Oxford's mortarboard, became popular. The tassel now worn is a stylized version of the tuft featured on some caps.

Caps and gowns have been worn in America since colonial times. In 1894, the Intercollegiate Commission standardized graduation attire in the United States.

Today, after the tassels have been turned and the caps

tossed, we pray our students will not see graduation as their educational end. Rather, we hope they will robe themselves in the joys of lifelong learning.

Show and Tell: If you still have your cap and gown, bring it to class and wear it for your kids; or, bring a graduation photo of yourself.

A Word with the "Principal": Wise God, thank you for occasions filled with pomp and circumstance! May I encourage the kids I teach to be lifelong students. Amen.

13. In Plenty and in Need

Object: *Chalk*

Theme: *Being a Resourceful Steward*

Textbook Reading: *Philippians 4:12-13 ~ In any and all circumstances I have learned the secret of . . . having plenty and of being in need. I can do all things through him who strengthens me.*

Lesson: While writing on the blackboard, the chalk suddenly crumbles in your hand, sending a shower of yellow dust onto your shirt. Oh, why can't your classroom have one of those wonderfully clean wipe-off boards?

Frustrated, you whirl around to grab another stick of chalk and your eyes sweep the room, taking in the ancient desks, the cracked linoleum floor tiles, the water stains on the ceiling, and the rust-flecked radiators. This school is so poor! How did you end up here?

Then the first bell rings, and a stream of students fills the room. Some scuffle in, looking as rundown as their surroundings; others bounce in, shining with energy and hope. Your heart goes out to each of them, and you remember why you are here: to teach, to reach, and to lift up these students.

As you look out at them, they look back at you and laugh. Once again, you realize that you are covered with chalk! You laugh with them, feeling a galvanizing of purpose. The second bell rings, the lesson begins, and God has strengthened you.

Group Work: Consider ways that your church family might support the needs of your school, such as providing classroom supplies or emergency lunch money.

A Word with the "Principal": Lord, help me to be resourceful in times of need, and strengthen my resolve to do all that I can with what I have. Amen.

14. A Time for Everything

Object: *Clocks*

Theme: *Marking and Using Time*

Textbook Reading: ***Ecclesiastes 3:3b ~ A time to break down and a time to build up.***

Lesson:

Tick, tock.

Every classroom has a clock, and each year the hours fly by as we work to set up our classrooms again. The walls are bare. The furniture stands in disarray. Empty shelves and cabinets await us. Boxes are piled by the door. There is much to be done.

We have often wished that we could just leave everything in place over the summer, but maintenance does need to clean the floors and paint the walls. Time after time, we pack up.

Breaking down the classroom sets a seal on the year gone by. It forces us to review the old and put aside what no longer seems best. Weeks later, when we reconstruct our classrooms for a new school year, we ready our minds and our materials for a new season with new students.

In the school year's cycle of beginnings and endings, may we remember that there is "a time for every matter under heaven" (Ecclesiastes 3:1).

Group Work: Try a "teacher trade table." After sorting through your classroom materials, bring those items you don't need any longer to a central location within the school. Enjoy swapping with others.

A Word with the "Principal": God of the ages, help me to make the most of every classroom minute! Amen.

15. Sticks and Stones

Object: *Erasers*

Theme: *Seeking Forgiveness*

Textbook Reading: ***Psalm 51:10 ~ Create in me a clean heart, O God, and put a new and right spirit within me.***

Lesson: "Sticks and stones will break my bones, but words will never hurt me."

Of course, we understand that this old saying is not true. Words do hurt. Just imagine the relief we would feel if we could erase all the hurtful words that we have ever uttered. All the discouraging words, cutting comments, destructive gossip, and pointless arguments would disappear from the memories of our colleagues, students, families, and acquaintances. Whose lives would be happier? Which relationships might be restored? How much more openly would we be received by others?

Unfortunately, we cannot erase what we have already said. We can, however, try to wipe the slate clean by telling those we have hurt that we are sorry. These words of contrition will begin a healing process for others as well as for ourselves.

Pop Quiz: Who stands in need of an apology from you? Allow God to work in your heart by asking those individuals for forgiveness.

A Word with the "Principal": Merciful God, help me to say I am sorry. Place in me a new and right spirit. Amen.

16. The Way

Object: *Hall Pass*

Theme: *Appreciating Our Freedom in Christ*

Textbook Reading: ***John 14:6a ~ Jesus said to him, "I am the way, and the truth, and the life."***

Lesson: Want to see a kid smile? Give a hall pass!

Many students relish the temporary freedom from classroom routine that a hall pass affords. Some kids equate a pass with a sense of privilege and feel honored by a teacher's trust. Others are delighted when a pass sends them on a special mission. Still others, quite honestly, are simply happy to have a break from class.

Because we Christians choose Jesus to be our teacher, we joyfully receive the "passes" he offers us. As our Savior, he grants us a unique freedom from the limits of this world. This cherished salvation is not an automatic right but a privilege we are honored to accept. And when we are filled with the love of Jesus, we are glad to be of service in his name.

There are times when we may stray from the path of hope, feeling bogged down and uninspired. Then may we remember that Jesus guides us and provides us with our "pass" to an extraordinary life.

Extra Credit: Surprise, reward, and empower your students this week by giving hall passes. Let them pick up books you have reserved at the media center, deliver a message to the office, or fetch a beverage for you from the cafeteria. Watch them smile!

A Word with the "Principal": Thank you, Lord, for the unique freedom that my faith in Jesus brings to me. Amen.

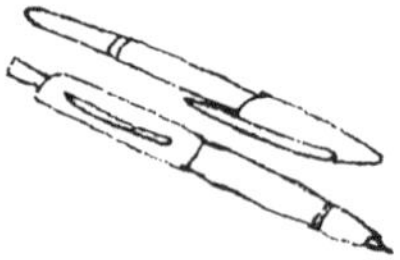

17. Tablets of Human Hearts

Object: *Pens*

Theme: *Communicating Genuine Care*

Textbook Reading: *2 Corinthians 3:3 ~ Show that you are a letter of Christ . . . written not with ink but with the Spirit of the living God, not on tablets of stone but on tablets of human hearts.*

Lesson: In the age of computerized student information systems, many of us work on our report cards at the keyboard. We no longer calculate grades by hand; nor do we pen comments about each student's progress. Instead, we make one or two selections from a list of over one hundred numbers, each representing comments such as "good student" or "does not use time wisely."

While this technology has lightened the workload, it also has depersonalized those reports to home. Be mindful that the old-fashioned, low-tech ways feel the most genuine and caring to students and their parents. A handwritten note of encouragement or concern speaks to their hearts. This year, let's try to pick up the pen for every one of our kids!

Show and Tell: Do you still have any handwritten notes from your teachers? Bring them in and show them to your students. Or, write a personalized note to a student today. You might even consider making this a regular habit!

A Word with the "Principal": Dear God, guide my hand as I write on the tablets of human hearts. Amen.

18. Ralph the Guinea Pig

Object: *Pets*

Theme: *Caring for God's Creatures*

Textbook Reading: ***Genesis 1:25 ~ God made the wild animals of the earth of every kind, and cattle of every kind, and everything that creeps upon the ground of every kind. And God saw that it was good.***

Lesson: Ralph was the teacher's pet—literally! When the teacher arrived every morning, Ralph recognized her footfalls, greeting her with excited cries of "Wheet, wheet." The teacher always brought the guinea pig a treat of fresh apples, carrots, or green beans. She was devoted to Ralph.

The kids were devoted to Ralph, too. He was a grand playmate, enjoying rides on the toy truck, deftly navigating the mazes the kids created, and snuggling into blankets when they played house.

It was a sad day when six-year-old Ralph died of a respiratory infection. Students from kindergarten through fifth grade were filled with grief, for Ralph was known to the whole school.

Any classroom from nursery school to high school becomes a more intriguing place when God's creatures are present. When we love and care for them, we come to appreciate their unique qualities and better understand the Creator's world.

Extra Credit: If you are unable to have a real animal for a classroom pet, consider a toy animal instead. Even older students will enjoy helping name the pet and determining his or her personality and habits. On weekends and holidays, students can take turns caring for the pet in their homes. And no parents will complain!

A *Word with the* "*Principal*": God of the ark, I ask your blessing on all the bright, beautiful, great, small, wise, and wonderful creatures of your earth. Amen.

19. The Work of Our Hands

Object: *Modeling Clay*

Theme: *Exercising Your Creativity*

Textbook Reading: ***Isaiah 64:8 ~ We are the clay, and you are our potter; we are all the work of your hand.***

Lesson: As young children, we had a splendid time playing with the colorful, pliant dough made with flour and salt. We kneaded, rolled, pinched, and shaped to our hearts content. Besides having fun and enhancing our gross motor skills, we also opened a door to our creativity.

When we grew older, our interests tuned to other things. We gave up the modeling of clay, using it only for the occasional science or history project. But perhaps we were too hasty. To keep their creativity flowing, many artists are advised to dabble in unfamiliar mediums and hobbies. The potter creates an oil painting. The painter tries a hand at writing. The writer throws a pot.

The mental challenge of attempting a different skill brings new perspectives and ideas. We teachers can learn lessons, too. After a long day or a long week, sculpting in clay, picking a guitar, or assembling a model may be just what we need. Although we are the work of God's hands, with marvelous combinations of talents, we can enliven these gifts by putting our hands to something new.

Extra Credit: Use modeling dough or clay as a warm-up activity with your kids. For math, ask them to make geometrical shapes. For English, let them fashion characters from stories they are writing. For social studies, they can create entire towns. Remember, even older children enjoy creating!

A Word with the "Principal": My Potter, shape me and enable me to be a creative teacher. Amen.

20. The Cure

Object: *Oral Thermometer*

Theme: *Cultivating a Curiosity for Learning*

Textbook Reading: *Luke 2:46 ~ After three days they found him [Jesus] in the temple, sitting among the teachers, listening to them and asking them questions.*

Lesson: "I feel sick. May I see the nurse?"

We eye our students carefully when they make this request. Who is ill? Who is faking it? Who wants to leave class because he or she is bored?

Some of these students who so eagerly want to leave class do not realize that they will never see this day again. They will not hear our lesson, and they will lose this opportunity to seek answers to timely questions. Textbooks offer much, but they cannot address a student face-to-face with definitions, explanations, clarifications, or elaboration.

Following a festival in Jerusalem, young Jesus was once among the missing. His parents found him three days later. But instead of avoiding school, Jesus was in the temple, asking his teachers amazing questions. He was certainly not a bored child.

"The cure for boredom is curiosity. There is no cure for curiosity," declared writer Ellen Parr.* If she is right, may an epidemic of curiosity sweep our schools and forever eliminate boredom!

Pop Quiz: What subject has aroused your curiosity lately? Do some exploring!

A *Word with the* "*Principal*": Clever God, help me to cultivate such a curiosity for learning in my students that they won't want to miss a single day of school! Amen.

---

*Ellen Parr quoted in "Quotable Quotes," *Reader's Digest,* December 1980.

21. Share the Faith

Object: *Flashcards*

Theme: *Sharing Your Faith*

Textbook Reading: *Ephesians 1:17 ~ I pray that the God of our Lord Jesus Christ, the Father of glory, may give you a spirit of wisdom and revelation as you come to know him.*

Lesson: Perhaps there are no greater moments in teaching than those times when we see a flash go off in the eyes of our students and we hear happy expressions such as, "Now I get it!" and "Oh, I see. That's easy!" and "Well, that makes sense!"

As Christians, sharing our faith with others isn't always as easy as sharing our knowledge with students. There aren't Christian flashcards. Yet we are called to be disciples of Jesus Christ.

Here are a few suggestions:

- Talk about your own faith and the impact it has on your life and your teaching.
- Speak in happy terms about your church life, even when you are weary from all your involvement.
- Invite folks to your church's worship service. If they seem hesitant, you might want to start with a potluck supper or the church bazaar.
- Let others know that you are praying for them.

Faith doesn't always come in a flash. As you share your faith, remember that good discipleship, just like good teaching, takes patience.

Extra Credit: One of the ways to become more comfortable sharing your faith is to think ahead of time what you might say. A helpful exercise is to practice expressing your faith is a sentence or two.

A Word with the "Principal": God of All People, give me the spirit of wisdom to share my faith. Amen.

22. Fire!

Object: ***Fire Alarm***

Theme: ***Recognizing That God Does Not Desert Us***

Textbook Reading: ***Psalm 23:4 ~ Even though I walk through the darkest valley, I fear no evil; for you are with me; your rod and your staff—they comfort me.***

Lesson:

The fire alarm!

Get into line, single file; no talking; turn off the lights; close the door.

And this isn't a scheduled fire drill. Could it be the real thing?

Watching over the lives and safety of our students can be a stressful responsibility, especially in these uncertain times. Even the calmest teacher has moments of sheer fear. They go along with the job. Bomb scares, gun violence, and natural threats such as tornadoes can put us to the test.

We may ask why these terrible things happen, but God doesn't promise us a life free from danger or fear. God does promise, however, not to desert us. In the darkest, scariest of times, God is with us. Through prayer, we can always communicate with God. We are not alone.

Extra Credit: Relief shelters offer comfort and assistance to victims of fire, many of whom are young children. Consider asking your class to donate boxes of crayons, drawing pads, and coloring books to be given to children who have lost their homes.

A Word with the "Principal": Holy Comforter, I thank you for being with me when life feels safe and when life feels scary. Amen.

23. Smile for the Camera

Object: *School Pictures*

Theme: *Looking into the Heart*

Textbook Reading: ***1 Samuel 16:7b ~ For the LORD does not see as mortals see; they look on the outward appearance, but the LORD looks on the heart.***

Lesson:

Picture day is one of those days of days for teachers each year.

There's the young lady who is despondent. She forgot this morning that it was picture day and she is wearing her drabbest turtleneck.

There's the young man who spills catsup on his clean white shirt.

There's another young lady in tears because her curls have fallen.

And there's the primping and the primping and the primping.

On picture day we are sometimes reminded that we live in a world that focuses on outward appearances.

How do we, as teachers, encourage our students to look at the heart? And how do we do a better job ourselves of getting beyond physical appearance—our own as well as that of others?

One simple way to move in this direction is to understand that God does not look at the outward appearance. God looks at the heart.

Extra Credit: As you look at your students this week, draw an imaginary heart next to their faces. Inside each heart, place a quality that makes that student endearing: cheerfulness, willingness to cooperate, a sense of fun, shyness, honesty, or enthusiasm.

A *Word with the* "Principal": Dear God, may I look not at the outward appearance of my students, but into their hearts. Amen.

24. In Paul's Footsteps

Object: *Staff ID*

Theme: *Reaching Out to Students*

Textbook Reading: *1 Corinthians 9:22b ~ I have become all things to all people.*

Lesson: The staff identification badges we wear are intended to label us as specific persons, backed by our personnel files in the administrative offices. However, our identity is not captured in a photo or confined to the pages in a folder. We are much more—to ourselves and to our students.

When Paul said, "I have become all things to all people," he was not speaking self-importantly. Rather, he was attempting to explain how he went about witnessing for Christ. By walking in the shoes of others, he was able to win them over to a belief in Jesus.

In our classrooms, we want to win our kids over to a belief in education. Like Paul, we can do this by having empathy for our students and by showing them that we have some understanding of who they are and how they perceive the world. To them, we represent education. Therefore, our effectiveness depends on whether they feel we care about them. Just as Paul offered hope to others through Jesus, so also we can offer hope to our students through education.

Pop Quiz: Which of your teachers seemed to care the most about you? How did this motivate and encourage you?

A Word with the "Principal": Lord, enable me, with insight and empathy, to reach out to my students. Amen.

25. Wonderful Words

Object: *The Dictionary*

Theme: *Contemplating Words of Faith*

Textbook Reading: *Psalm 119:105 ~ Your word is a lamp to my feet and a light to my path.*

Lesson:

Definitions. That's a word that will make older students cringe. Kids grow tired of looking up vocabulary word after vocabulary word. It takes an innovative teacher to come up with ways to make the dictionary intriguing.

But what an intriguing book the dictionary really is: pages upon pages of words. Sometimes it's fun to let your fingers walk down a column and stop on a single word.

The Bible is made up of words, too—the wonderful words of our Christian faith: *alleluia, garden, Jesus, neighbor, cross, forgiveness, creation, dove, mercy, miracle, disciple, savior, believe, twelve, peace, gospel, hope, love.* Take the Bible apart word by word and you will find key words that teach, inspire, encourage, and enlighten. Sometimes thinking about one word can be more meaningful than reading hundreds of them. As you study the scriptures, occasionally focus your thoughts on a single word and its significance to your faith.

Show and Tell: Students of all ages love to play "Word of the Day." When they hear the word, they are to raise their hands, clap, say the word back, or give some other signal that the class has decided upon.

A Word with the "Principal": Dear God, words here, words there, words everywhere. Thank you for words, especially the words of my faith. Amen.

26. Settling into Prayer

Object: *Nap Mats*

Theme: *Needing Prayer Time*

Textbook Reading: ***Matthew 6:6 ~ But whenever you pray, go into your room and shut the door and pray to your Father who is in secret; and your Father who sees in secret will reward you.***

Lesson: Isn't it wonderful when we finally have our students settled into a routine? Once they know what to expect, their minds and bodies become comfortable and responsive. They listen to stories or lessons, actively participate during math and science and music, and rest or work quietly when it's naptime or quiet time.

We, too, move through our day more easily if we have a routine. Our great challenge is finding the time to do all we need and want to do. We must work, eat, and sleep. We should run errands, exercise, keep up with family and friends, and so many other things. There's one thing in particular we need to do that often gets pushed aside. What? Pray.

Yes, we need time each day to nourish our spirits—a quiet time, a time set within our daily routine. Consider a commitment to pray each day in a specific place for fifteen minutes. This will establish a pattern. As we grow accustomed to this prayer time, our bodies and minds will settle down and we'll be ready to focus. After a few weeks, our spirits will reap the rewards, and a designated prayer time will be a treasured habit.

Show and Tell: It's difficult to pray "in secret", as Matthew 6:6 advises, when a family member or roommate is around. Request fifteen minutes of peace and quiet and explain where and when you will be praying. Your example may inspire others!

A *Word with the* "*Principal*": God, grant me firmness of resolve and patience with myself and others as I settle into a pattern of daily prayer. Amen.

27. Children of Light

Object: *Calculator*

Theme: *Making a Difference in the World*

Textbook Reading: *John 12:35b-36 ~ If you walk in the darkness you do not know where you are going. While you have the light, believe in the light, so that you may become children of light.*

Lesson: How can we possibly calculate and comprehend all the far-reaching consequences of our actions? When we remember the not-so-nice things we've done or said, it's like sliding down a dark and chilly tunnel with no end in sight. Conversely, when we reflect upon our good deeds, works of kindness, and acts of love, we are aglow with warmth and light.

It's an age-old question: Why do we give in to the forces of darkness within us when behaving as children of light feels vastly better? The simplest answer is to say we have an imperfect nature, distorted by selfishness and fear. The human tendency for skepticism and doubt can cause us to teeter on a pinnacle of apathy and inaction. However, when we allow God to work within our flawed souls, we do have a great capacity for generosity, faith, courage, and caring.

In the book and movie *Pay It Forward,* the result of a teacher's assignment encourages us to believe that we can make a difference in the world. If we claim our heritage as children of God, flooding the darkness of our hearts with God's light, then we will multiply the possibilities for peace, grace, and joy in our world.

Show and Tell: Explain to your class the concept of paying it forward: One person helps three people in significant ways and those three people each promise to help three more. An unending chain of goodness is begun!

A *Word with the* "*Principal*": Holy God, you have given me blessings beyond calculation. Show me how to send them forward. Amen.

28. Oh, Those Earthly Treasures

Object: *Lockers*

Theme: *Recognizing Nonmaterial Treasures*

Textbook Reading: Matthew 6:19 ~ ***Do not store up for yourselves treasures on earth, where moth and rust consume and where thieves break in and steal.***

Lesson: What treasures a locker can hold: a Christmas doll, resting until Show and Tell; a leather jacket, a birthday present from Grandma; a baseball glove, perfect for catching fly balls at recess.

Kids love their treasures. And loving treasures is part of loving life. The jacket speaks of the affection of a grandmother; the baseball glove represents the thrill of the game; and the doll certainly calls for a good mother.

But how do we temper—in ourselves and in our students—the love of possessions with more significant values in life? At times, this can be a daunting task. Sharing what we have, emphasizing the nonmaterial, giving through service, and offering thoughtful prayers are good ways to start.

Now about the constant slamming of those locker doors . . .

Group Work: Help your students understand that not all treasures are material possessions by putting out slips of paper and a pretty box to serve as the Treasure Chest. Over the course of a week, let kids write down some of their nonmaterial treasures: the name of a favorite aunt; a compliment they have received; a favor happily returned from a friend. Consider reading the treasures aloud at the end of the week. Or, with older students, have them write poems, essays, or skits about their nonmaterial treasures.

A *Word with the* "*Principal*": God of Earth and Heaven, I thank you for the joys of this world as I await your treasure in heaven. Amen.

29. The Writing on the Wall

Object: *Murals*

Theme: *Writing Graffiti*

Textbook Reading: ***Romans 15:4 ~ For whatever was written in former days was written for our instruction, so that by steadfastness and by the encouragement of the scriptures we might have hope.***

Lesson: Most kids from eighteen months to eighteen years have experienced the urge to mark on walls. From primitive cave drawings to twenty-first-century-street graffiti, people have depicted or written about many things that have touched their lives.

The Italian word *graffiti* means "a scratching," and there is plenty of evidence of it in Pompeii. During the excavations of ruins, graffiti was found cut into pillars, walls, and doorposts. The name of a tavern keeper, the latest scandal, and pictures of gladiators were among the findings. Even more interesting is the graffiti in the catacombs of Rome, where Christians sought refuge. There, in tunnels reaching from twenty-five to sixty-five feet below ground, these believers worshiped and scratched out the stories of early Christian life and doctrine.

Today we can channel the talents of our graffiti artists by stretching paper across a wall and inviting kids to paint, write poetry, draw cartoons, editorialize, joke, question, or simply sign in. While kids like the free space, they will find more academic murals to be fun too. Target specific historical periods and places, asking kids to respond as residents of that day to discoveries, politics, literature, and art. Give your group a constructive outlet: Create a graffiti wall.

Pop Quiz: Tell the truth! Have you ever written graffiti?

A Word with the "Principal": Thank you, Lord, for graffiti, radio waves, books, CDs, magazines, and TV screens that spread the Good News. Amen.

30. Showing Honor

Object: *The Honor Roll*

Theme: *Recognizing Academic Stress*

Textbook Reading: ***Romans 12:10 ~ Love one another with mutual affection; outdo one another in showing honor.***

Lesson: Seeing their names on the honor roll is exciting for students. When they are young, kids are just as glad to see their friends' names on the list, too. Unfortunately, as students progress to middle and high school, an edgy competition often arises between them. Jockeying for class rank and challenging one another for awards, distinctions, and scholarships creates stress. These pressures can push some to take desperate measures in their quest for an extra point here or an advantage there. Even the less obsessive students sometimes experience anxiety, depression, and fatigue because of it.

Of course, we cannot control our driven students, their often-demanding parents, or the ever-rising expectations of college admissions boards. Thankfully, there are some things we can do within our own sphere of influence. First, we can conduct ourselves honorably, thereby creating a safety zone for our kids. If we don't show favoritism or disrespect or set one student against another, and if we always offer clarity and consistency in assignments and evaluations, our students will benefit.

Second, by working with students to establish an honor code, we will teach them that personal integrity is more essential to their well-being than winning at any cost. Let's help them recognize that external measurements of achievements are only part of the equation for happiness and success.

***Group Work*:** Discuss your school's honor code with your students. If none exists, generate one together for use in your classroom.

A *Word with the* "*Principal*": Dear God, may I foster honor and integrity in my students. Amen.

31. Time-Out!

Object: *Time-Out Chair*

Theme: *Taking Time to Find the Cause of Problems*

Textbook Reading: ***Ezra 10:4 ~ Take action, for it is your duty, and we are with you; be strong, and do it.***

Lesson: Here's what one elementary teacher says about the time-out chair:

Cheating. Spitting. Lying. Back talking. Hitting. Stealing. Cursing. Tripping. All these and any other acts of negative intent will land the guilty in my time-out chair.

No innocent smiles, angelic eyes, slumped shoulders, wringing hands, or hasty apologies will spare my kids this experience. I have no desire to spurn or ridicule. What I seek is the cause of their behavior.

After the child in the chair has had time to calm down and reflect, he or she knows that I, too, will take a "time-out" to listen to the problem. Sometimes this one-to-one talk leads to a simple solution. Other times, it may uncover more deeply rooted issues. In all circumstances, though, it is better to take action and do my duty by each student than to turn a weary eye away from these situations. It's a challenge to stay strong amid the daily skirmishes and their underlying causes, but with the help of the Holy Spirit and the support of parents, colleagues, and administrators, I can do it.

Extra Credit: Don't have a time-out chair? Consider encouraging your kids to visit you during your planning period, lunch, or recess to share what's on their minds. Take the time to be a good listener!

A Word with the "Principal": Triune God, I ask to be guided and empowered by the Holy Spirit as I deal with behavior problems. Amen.

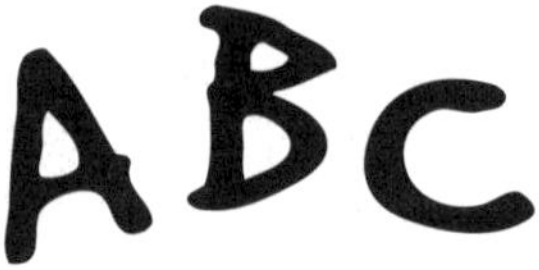

32. Lines and Squiggles

Object: *The Alphabet*

Theme: *Needing Jesus*

Textbook Reading: ***Revelation 22:13~ I am the Alpha and the Omega, the first and the last, the beginning and the end.***

Lesson:

Lines and squiggles made twenty-six ways,
Turn into words before our gaze!
(from a poem by Barbara Younger)

It's really rather amazing that those lines and squiggles give us written language. Without written language, we would be lost: no books, no letters, no prescriptions, no recipes, no road signs, no diaries, and no birthday cards!

The alphabet was important in Jesus' day, too. In John's book of Revelation, Jesus uses the first and the last letters of the Greek alphabet to make his point: "I am the Alpha and the Omega." Jesus will be with us always, from the beginning to the end, from A to Z. Without Jesus, we would surely feel lost.

And thanks to those lines and squiggles arranged in twenty-six different ways, we can read the words of Jesus, our Savior, from our very own Bibles.

Show and Tell: Creating alphabet books is a great language enrichment skill for older students. After showing your class a few time-tested favorites as well as some of the newly published alphabet books, challenge them to create their own. Even middle school and high school students will enjoy choosing creative themes and illustrating their books. You may want to have them present, or send, their finished books to a class of younger students.

A *Word with the* "Principal": A, B, C, D, E, F, G . . . Lord, I'm glad you sent Jesus to be with me! Amen.

33. At the Crossroads

Object: *Bus*

Theme: *Seeking Advice and Understanding*

Textbook Reading: *Jeremiah 6:16a ~ Stand at the crossroads, and look, and ask for the ancient paths, where the good way lies.*

Lesson: The wheels of the bus go round and round—except when they come to a screeching stop at the crossroads of our career path, the road of a relationship, our spiritual journey, or the street where our health, finances, old habits, and new dreams reside. We know we have to make our own way in the world, but let's remember that we don't have to go it alone. There are sage and well-traveled people on the bus with us right now. When some advice or understanding is needed, we may turn to those who have been down the road before us.

Although the problems we solve, the choices we make, the situations we navigate, and the issues we contemplate are extremely personal, they are not unique to human experience. For us, there are shoulders to lean on, ears to listen, and voices to share wisdom. As we stand at the crossroads, we'll find someone to ask where the good way lies.

Group Work: If you are currently at a crossroad, consider consulting with a person or support group to help you with this passage. If you feel unable to face anyone yet, consider reading faith-based books on the topic that is troubling you.

A Word with the "Principal": Be with me, O God, at every cross in the road. Amen.

34. Love Is . . .

Object: *School Glue*

Theme: **Making** ***Our Lives Stronger with Love***

Textbook Reading: ***1 Corinthians 13:4-7 ~ Love is patient; love is kind; love is not envious or boastful or arrogant or rude. It does not insist on its own way; it is not irritable or resentful; it does not rejoice in wrongdoing but rejoices in the truth. It bears all things, believes all things, hopes all things, endures all things.***

Lesson: Let's pretend. Our summer assignment is to make a scrapbook of our lives. We are given a giant book, lots of glue, and six weeks of time.

What would we choose to fill the pages? Many of our favorite memories, of course, captured in clippings, photographs, programs, cards, certificates, and other mementos. And what is the primary emotion these keepsakes reflect? Love. The love of others for us; our love for others and ourselves; and the evidence of God's love in our lives. What greater glue is there?

Through love, we bear up under the stress of daily living, believe in God's mercy and justice, hope for and celebrate life's goodness, and endure all the troubling or tragic events that come along. When we think of our priorities, the things worth doing and worth remembering, let's not pretend. Let's make our lives stronger with love.

Extra Credit: Do you have a shoebox full of mementos? It's time to make a keepsake scrapbook for yourself or a loved one. Use acid-free paper and nonyellowing glue to preserve photos, clippings, and other mementos in the best fashion. This can be a fun family project or a great way to get closer to a friend. Let the video camera run while you work. The laughter and stories are worth playing back!

A *Word with the* "*Principal*": Dear God, I'm grateful for the scraps of love that form the book of my life. Amen.

35. Count Those Days!

Object: *Calendars*

Theme: *Making Each Day Count*

Textbook Reading: ***Psalm 90:12 ~ So teach us to count our days that we gain a wise heart.***

Lesson: Who doesn't enjoy a crisp new calendar at the start of a brand new year? Flip the pages to see all the months and weeks and days that lie ahead. But alas, soon that lovely, clean calendar will be filled with appointments and obligations. Before long, we'll look at the calendar and sigh. We're just too busy.

How do we keep our days from going by so fast that we can't even count them? To gain a wise heart, surely we must, as teachers, take time to smell the playground or school campus in the early spring, taste the birthday cupcakes or the occasional goodies in the teacher's lounge, see the improvements in a student's work, touch the moss in the classroom terrarium, and hear the laughter of students on a giddy morning. To count our days we must appreciate them and all the small joys that they bring us.

One teacher took her new calendar and marked every few days with asterisks. On those days she was to make certain she paused, even if just for a moment, to appreciate her day. Sometimes she said a word of prayer; other times she enjoyed a candy from her drawer or a few minutes at the open window. Some days she only had a moment for a good deep breath. But it was a breath that said, I am alive and this is my day!

Extra Credit: Even if you aren't one to keep a journal or diary, try for at least a week to jot on your calendar one moment in your day that was especially touching or meaningful.

***A Word with the* "Principal":** O God, our help in ages past and our hope for years to come, may I appreciate this day! Amen.

36. Our Spinning Planet

Subject: *The Globe*

Theme: *Appreciating God's Task*

Textbook Reading: ***Job 38:4 ~ Where were you when I laid the foundation of the earth? Tell me, if you have understanding.***

Lesson: The next time you spin a globe or look at a world map, pretend that you are God creating and caring for the earth. It makes teaching seem like an easy job, doesn't it?

We can't really put ourselves into God's shoes, and perhaps it is presumptuous to even try. Yet by imagining what it might be like to be the creator and sustainer of the earth, we are humbled and awed by the magnitude of God's task.

Our friend Job got himself in a bit of trouble by questioning God. God answers Job out of the whirlwind using some of the most expansive and magnificent language of the Bible:

> "Where were you when I laid the foundation of the earth . . .
> Have you commanded the morning since your days began?
> Have you entered into the springs of the sea? . . .
> Have you entered the storehouses of the snow . . . ?
> Do you know when the mountain goats give birth? . . . "
> (Job 38:4, 12, 16, 22; 39:1)

What a world! What a responsibility! Thank you, God.

Extra Credit: When you get a moment alone in your classroom or at home, spin a globe, with one finger resting on it. When it stops, check and see where in the world your finger is. Say a word of prayer for the people who live in that place.

A *Word with the* "*Principal*": God of the spinning planets, bless you for caring for the earth and all the earth's inhabitants. Amen.

37. Into the Future

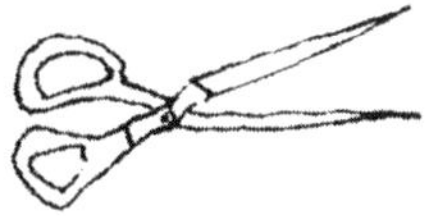

Object: *Scissors*

Theme: *Considering Our Students' Futures*

Textbook Reading: ***Proverbs 23:18 ~ Surely there is a future, and your hope will not be cut off.***

Lesson: The mastery of scissors is quite the preschool and kindergarten challenge. As children learn to cut, not many think about the fact that they will use scissors over and over again in the years to come. Actually, although they like to think about getting older and growing up, few young children put serious thought into their future.

But as teachers, the futures of our students are a serious concern. That's why we teach. We want to help our students cut out tomorrows for themselves that are happy and fulfilling. One of the ways that we can do this is by assuring all our students that they have futures of promise. As teachers, we must empower our kids to see beyond the limits of family backgrounds, test scores, physical and emotional problems, and economic hardships. Especially as children grow older and enter the preteen and teen years, this can be a challenge. We have our work cut out for us.

Group Work: Since its invention, artists have cut paper into interesting shapes and designs. Kids of any age will enjoy taking a turn at this form of self-expression. The next time a bulletin board is empty or a display needs to be assembled, pass out scissors and paper, and then announce a theme or give instructions. Watch your "snippers" demonstrate their creativity.

A Word with the "Principal": Dear God, guide my hands, my mind, and my heart as I help my students prepare for their futures. Amen.

38. Circle of Believers

Object: *Compass*

Theme: *Meditating on the Cross*

Textbook Reading: ***Hebrews 12:2 ~ Looking to Jesus, the pioneer and perfecter of our faith, who for the sake of the joy that was set before him endured the cross, disregarding its shame, and has taken his seat at the right hand of the throne of God.***

Lesson: With a compass, we are able to scribe a circle. This circle may begin a picture book, illustrate a story problem, help solve an experiment, launch an adventure in map making, or form the symbol for "no" with a diagonal line drawn through it. With imagination, intellect, and tools we can transform a circle into many things.

The cross, however, is something only Jesus could transform. In his day, it was an abhorrent image; but this sign of a tortured and degrading death was forever changed by the Savior's Resurrection. Now it is a sacred image to his followers. Christians worship the One represented by the cross, wear the cross, and welcome the sign of the cross in their communities. For Christians, the cross is an offering of God's grace and love, a sign of strength and power, and the symbol of faith. We are part of an ever-growing circle of believers who trust in the love of Jesus and his offer of a new life.

Extra Credit: Give a friend or family member a gift of a cross necklace, tie tack, earrings, or lapel pin. Share with that person what the cross means to you.

A Word with the "Principal": God of the cross, encircle me with your grace as I ask forgiveness for my sins. Amen.

39. Serendipity!

Object: *Lesson Plan Book*

Theme: *Recognizing the Working of the Holy Spirit in the Classroom*

Textbook Reading: ***Proverbs 16:3 ~ Commit your work to the Lord, and your plans will be established.***

Lesson: We all know what can happen to the greatest plans of mice and men and teachers. They can go awry.

Of course, good teaching involves planning, but there are times when, praise God, serendipity takes over our classrooms: the class ham's impromptu impersonation of Patrick Henry, or the discovery of a chrysalis on the window that the class can observe each day until a butterfly emerges.

One dictionary defines serendipity as "the gift of finding valuable or agreeable things not sought for."* Such a happy sounding word for a happy element of life. There is even a "serendipity berry." This African berry boasts a protein that is many times sweeter than sugar. The berry's amazing sweetness was discovered quite by accident, hence its name.

Some might call serendipity just happenstance or luck. Christians might call it the sweet grace of the Holy Spirit working in the classroom. Enjoy it!

Pop Quiz: Recall some recent moments of serendipity in your classroom.

A Word with the "Principal": God, for moments of serendipity caused by the working of your Holy Spirit in my classroom, I say a heartfelt "hooray!" Amen.

---

*From *Webster's New Collegiate Dictionary*, G. and C. Merriam Co., 1972.

40. A Need for Feedback

Object: *Report Cards*

Theme: *Keeping in Touch with Personal Progress*

Textbook Reading: *Matthew 7:7 ~ Ask, and it will be given you; search, and you will find; knock, and the door will be opened for you.*

Lesson: Interim reports, grading period reports, semester and end-of-year reports—all are designed to keep teachers, parents, and students current with school progress. We hope that our individual evaluations generate an active interest from parents and a positive response from students.

We believe this feedback is good for our students, so how might we fare if we received a monthly report on our own status? In the subjects of family, friends, church, community, self-care, work, and play, what would our grades be?

Perhaps we would feel discouraged if we didn't make all A's. More likely, we would find it valuable to have an early warning of when we are getting off balance or some reassurance that we are doing well. We would like encouragement when we've managed to shed those unwanted pounds or a caution when we're not acting like ourselves; consolation as we head into a crisis and a tip when we're stuck in a problem at school.

There are people around us who can say the words we need to hear. First we must open the door to our own willingness. Next, we must seek out a few trusted friends and begin to regularly ask for their observations and opinions on how we are managing our lives.

Report cards from friends? Don't knock this idea until you've tried it!

***Show and Tell*:** Be brave: pass around some of your old report cards to show your kids. Invite parents to send in theirs, too!

A *Word with the* "*Principal*": Lord, because my state of mind and my actions affect many other people, help me to receive the feedback I need to grow in goodness. Amen.

41. By Our Love

Object: *The Flag*

Theme: *Living Out Faith in the Classroom*

Textbook Reading: *Psalm 20:5 ~ May we shout for joy over your victory, and in the name of God set up our banners.*

Lesson:

You're a grand old flag,
You're a high flying flag . . .

The flag is displayed proudly in many classrooms in our country, but there are no crosses mounted in our public schools. We who teach cannot openly set up banners to God since we live in a nation that subscribes to the separation of church and state.

Most Christian educators understand that this is one of our fundamental national principles. So, how do we bring our faith into our work as teachers without violating the separation of church and state?

One second grade teacher writes:

> God provides many opportunities for witnessing in the classroom. I believe that we are always an example for Christ in the way that we treat our students and respond to their needs. Patience and understanding go a long way. God places opportunities before us every day. We need to be aware of them and respond the way God would expect us to.

While she doesn't wave a Christian flag or a cross in front of her students, this teacher uses her faith every day in her work with children. And so do you!

Group Work: Let the students create a class flag for the room or the hallway. Before kids begin to draw on cotton fabric with markers or crayons, have them discuss symbols and slogans that represent the character and purpose of their class. Then proudly display that grand new flag!

A *Word with the* "*Principal*": Dear God, may I be a witness to the love of Jesus in my teaching. Amen.

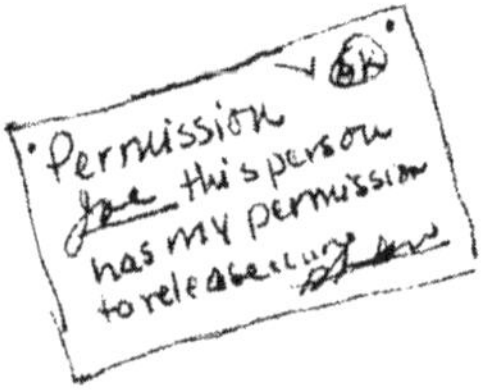

42. The Field Is the World

Object: *Permission Slip*

Theme: *Taking Field Trips*

Textbook Reading: *Matthew 13:38 ~ The field is the world, and the good seed are the children of the kingdom.*

Lesson: "Travel, in the younger sort, is part of education." These words were written by essayist and philosopher Francis Bacon (1561–1626) long ago.

As teachers of this new century, most of us agree with Mr. Bacon. If we know that field trips are important, why then are we sometimes hesitant to schedule them? And why is the happiest moment of a field trip often when the bus pulls into the school parking lot at the end of the day?

Because field trips are nerve-wracking. There's the bus with the flat tire; the student who brings the contraband water pistol; the catcalls during the planetarium show; and the cartwheels in the art museum. Of course, we can add the gift shop, rain, lost spending money, upset stomachs, and worst of all, the head count that reveals two students are missing. With older students, there is a completely new set of challenges.

Take heart. God must endorse travel, too, because the Bible is filled with journeys. Imagine the field trips of Bible days: cold nights in the desert, the search for water, dusty roads, and the lack of both restaurants and powder rooms. And then there's one of the most famous field trips of all times: *"We three kings of Orient are; bearing gifts we traverse afar, field and fountain, moor and mountain . . . "*

Be brave. Schedule your next field trip. And Godspeed to you all!

Group Work: Go on a few more field trips each year by taking them in your classroom. Choose a destination and let decorations, snacks, music, artifacts, and vivid imaginations turn your classroom into a fabulous field trip destination. Even older students love this!

A Word with the "Principal": God of all travelers, thank you for the opportunities I have to show my students a bit of the world. Amen.

43. The Fun Stuff!

Object: *Intercom*

Theme: *Exhibiting a Fun Spirit*

Textbook Reading: *Isaiah 28:23-24*a ~ *Listen, and hear my voice; pay attention, and hear my speech. Do those who plow for sowing plow continually?*

Lesson: What is everyone's favorite part of the morning announcements? It's certainly not a scolding about dress code violations or the reminder about yearbook fees. It's the fun stuff! We want to hear about the debut of the new uniforms at tonight's game, the upcoming carnival, or the big dance next week. Our school is a community, and these events are our time to socialize and celebrate.

Consequently, when we put aside our fatigue or demanding schedules to lead some cheers at the game; to serve as a water balloon target at the dunking booth; or to shake a leg at the school dance, our students absolutely love it. They delight in seeing us step out of our classroom persona. They are amazed to spot us with our spouse or children, or even our dog. Students consider it a major news event if a teacher is sighted at the mall or in a restaurant, especially if the teacher waves a hand or speaks a greeting. To our students, we are indeed special.

As teachers, we are expected to plow the rich soil of our students' minds, but not continuously. From time to time, they need us simply to join in the fun.

Pop Quiz: Which of your teachers was the most fun outside of the classroom. Why?

A Word with the "Principal": God of Joy, spark us with the spirit of fun. Amen.

44. Special Delivery

Object: *Bulletin Board*

Theme: *Spreading Good News*

Textbook Reading: ***Romans 10:15b ~ How beautiful are the feet of those who bring good news!***

Lesson: The Scripture does not say, How beautiful is the face or the voice of those who bring good news.

Instead, it refers to the person's *feet.* Why? In Bible times, breaking news was delivered to a household, government office, or the town's gathering place by a messenger on foot. War, hailstorm damage to crops, or spreading illness were dreaded but vital pieces of information. In contrast, news of peace, abundant harvest, or a birth were most welcome. Oh, how beautiful were the dusty and callused feet of the bearer of those good tidings.

In today's information age, our messengers are the radio, television, newspaper, telephone, and Internet. Technology has become the "feet" that deliver the news. We can be bombarded with negative signs, sounds, and stories at all hours and from all around the world.

One way to shift the emphasis from the stressful to the joyful is to designate a Good News Bulletin Board in your classroom. Encourage or assign students to find and share stories with a positive perspective; then have them post them on the board. Your messengers will feel beautiful from the top of their heads to the bottom of their feet.

Show and Tell: Take the lead by showing, telling, and posting the kinds of stories, announcements, and photos you want the kids to collect. The bulletin board should be a forum for students to post their personal good news, too. Invite them to write brief articles of good news about themselves.

A *Word with the* "Principal": We praise you, Lord, for the eternally good news of our salvation through Jesus. Amen.

45. Hungry?

Object: *Lunch Box*

Theme: *Finding a Way to Share Lunch*

Textbook Reading: ***Hebrews 13:16 ~ Do not neglect to do good and to share what you have, for such sacrifices are pleasing to God.***

Lesson:

Top two reasons to bring your lunch:
  Liking what you will have to eat.
  No waiting in the cafeteria line.
Top two reasons not to bring your lunch:
  It can be lost or stolen.
  It can get squished.
Top two reasons to share your lunch:
  Someone shows up without a lunch box.
  Someone has no lunch money.

With a Pavlovian response, kids are ready and eager to eat when they hear the bell ring. For most, it's the highlight of their school day. However, we've seen the sad or anxious faces of those students who have forgotten their money or their lunch boxes, or had them stolen.

Some schools remedy this situation by allowing students to charge their lunch in the cafeteria. Whether your school does this or not, here's an alternative idea. Invite your kids to contribute a package of their favorite nonperishable lunch box foods such as drinks, chips, fruit and dessert cups, and snacks with some protein such as peanut butter crackers or microwavable soups. You provide the paper lunch bags, plastic forks and spoons, and a verminproof cabinet or storage box to keep the foods safe.

Together, your students can have the fun of creating a collection of emergency bag lunches. Your plan for sharing not only will please God, but it also will please your kids.

Extra Credit: Collect items to make emergency lunch bags for kids arriving in safe houses and shelters, or for families who use the local food bank.

A *Word with the* "Principal": Lord, may we not neglect to share our food with those who are hungry. Amen.

46. Getting the Picture

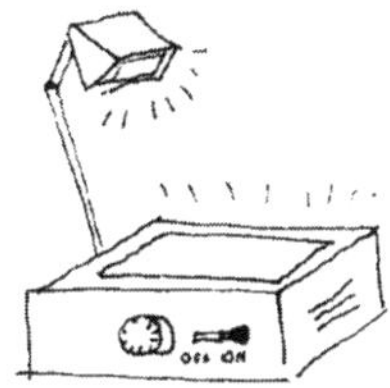

Object: *Overhead Projector*

Theme: *Focusing on the Good Things*

Textbook Reading: ***Colossians 2:17 ~ These are only a shadow of what is to come, but the substance belongs to Christ.***

Lesson: Kids will only give you a few seconds before they begin to call, "Focus! Focus!"

An overhead projector is a useful teaching tool, but occasionally the focus is off. It's not unusual for our own focus to need adjustment, too. When times of gloominess or frustration cloud our vision, we can have trouble seeing the goodness in the world and in ourselves.

On difficult days, it's best for us not to project the world's troubles inward or to project our negativity onto others. Naturally, we are affected by external circumstances, and we should not bottle up our feelings; but there is a difference between reacting and being overwrought. Achieving a balance can be easier when we value the good we see in others, count even the smallest blessing, and appreciate life's small celebrations and victories.

All the goodness around us is merely a shadow of what is to come to us through Jesus Christ.

Extra Credit: When you're feeling sad or grumpy, try this: for the next day, focus on good thoughts, good people, good events, good feelings, and good works. See how much happier you are.

A Word with the "Principal": Living Lord, let your Spirit fall afresh on me. Amen.

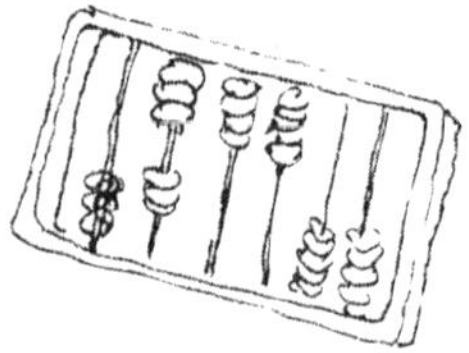

47. What Counts?

Object: *Abacus*

Theme: *Thinking About What Is Really Important*

Textbook Reading: *Genesis 15:5*a ~ *He brought him outside and said, "Look toward heaven and count the stars, if you are able to count them."*

Lesson: Physicist Albert Einstein, one of the greatest minds ever to grace the earth, had this to say about counting: "Not everything that counts can be counted. Not everything that can be counted counts."*

So what counts?

Stuart Little, one of the greatest mouse minds ever to grace children's literature, takes a turn at substitute teaching in E. B. White's beloved classic. Stuart asks one of the students, Harry Rackmeyer, to tell the class what is important. Harry responds, "A shaft of sunlight at the end of a dark afternoon, a note in music, and the way the back of a baby's neck smells if its mother keeps it tidy."**

To this fine list, Mary Bendix adds ice cream with chocolate sauce on it.

So what else is important?

Deciding what counts and what is important is integral to our work as teachers and our life as Christians. The Bible gives us guidelines, but the rest is up to us. Contemplation, observation, evaluation, study, experience, optimism, generosity, and prayer can lead us toward understanding what really counts and what is really important.

And thanks to Mr. Einstein and Mr. Little for their insights!

Group Work: Students of all ages will appreciate the wisdom of Stuart Little. Use chapter 12, "The Schoolroom," to begin a discussion and a list of what your students think is really important.

A *Word with the* "Principal": All wise and knowing God, guide me toward a genuine understanding of what counts and what is important. Amen.

---

*Albert Einstein quoted in *2002 Guideposts for Teens Calendar,* Guideposts, P.O. Box 1437, Carmel, N.Y. 10512.

**E. B. White, *Stuart Little,* Harper Bros. Publishers, 1945, p. 94.

48. A Mighty Tall Tower

Object: *Blocks*

Theme: *Building Community in the Classroom*

Textbook Reading: *Ephesians 2:22 ~ In whom you also are built together spiritually into a dwelling place for God.*

Lesson:

Building community.

How do we get kids from twenty-five different homes to live as one community in our classroom? How do we keep jealousy and pettiness and mistrust and behavior problems and plain old personality clashes from knocking down those towers of love and learning over and over again?

There is no simple solution. Just as families and churches don't always live as one community, neither do students. Here are few building blocks to help steady your foundation.

Work and play together. Group games and projects create enthusiasm and team spirit. But don't forget to champion individual opinions and interests. Set and share class goals and concerns. But leave time each week for students to voice their personal quests and problems. Mix kids up, assign new partners, switch the groups. But honor the freedom to choose friends and to be alone, too.

Thriving families, churches, and classrooms value the spirit of each individual while, at the same time, they work together to create a cohesive community.

What a mighty tall tower a box of blocks can build!

Group Work: Your students will enjoy creating edible towers. Have them work in teams to create towers using peanut butter and crackers of various shapes. Once constructed and admired, towers make scrumptious snacks. Even older kids will find this a delectable challenge.

A Word with the "Principal": God, my foundation and cornerstone, may I use the building blocks of love, patience, creativity, and wisdom to construct community in my classroom. Amen.

49. Happy Birthday to You

Object: *Cupcakes*

Theme: *Celebrating Yourself*

Textbook Reading: *Psalm 139:13 ~ For it was you who formed my inward parts; you knit me together in my mother's womb.*

Lesson: "Are you one? Are you two? Are you three? Are you four? Are you five? Are you six? Are you seven? Are you eight? Are you nine?"

In some places, it's the custom for kids to chant these questions, adding another year each time until the birthday child shouts, "Stop!"

For kids, there's nothing like adding another year to their age.

We teachers are perhaps a bit less enthusiastic about adding another year to our age, but we still love birthdays. (And those cupcakes are so delicious.)

The Bible tells us that God knew who we were even before we were born. God has been our God since our first spark of life. God created us and knit us together in our mother's wombs. And so, when we become discouraged with ourselves, we must remember that we are a part of God's mighty plan. We are God's creation, every bit of us. One aspect of loving God is loving and respecting ourselves—faults and imperfections included.

So, pat yourself on the back. Forgive yourself. Congratulate yourself. Indulge yourself. Pamper yourself. Celebrate life. Celebrate yourself. Have two cupcakes!

Show and Tell: Most young children can barely fathom that their teachers were once babies, and older kids wonder what you must have looked like. Prove to them that indeed you were a baby once, and a darling one at that.

Bring in baby photos, your baby album, and other treasures of your early years to share with your class.

A *Word with the* "*Principal*": Dear God, for cupcakes and children and birthdays and plain old me, may I be truly thankful. Amen.

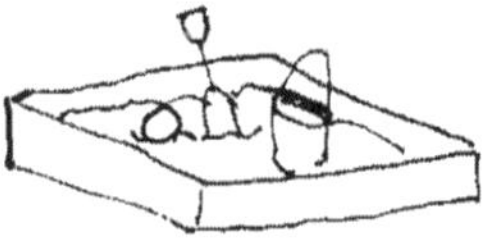

50. Building on Solid Rock

Object: *Sandbox*

Theme: *Building a Foundation of Faith*

Textbook Reading: *Matthew 7:26-27 ~ And everyone who hears these words of mine and does not act on them will be like a foolish man who built his house on sand. The rain fell, and the floods came, and the winds blew, and beat against the house, and it fell—and great was its fall!*

Lesson: Playing in the sand is a pleasant pastime. Sand, a fluid and forgiving medium, is quickly carved into a tunnel bridge for toy trucks, molded into a fancy castle, or crafted into a turtle or a sophisticated sand sculpture. Sandboxes, sand tables, and beaches provide hours of fun for kids of all ages.

The qualities of sand that make it easy for kids to work with are also the qualities that make their creations only temporary. The tunnel bridge caves in, the castle is scored by wind, and the sculpture is eroded by the rain.

We can compare sand to the material possessions we use to build our lives. A new truck, an addition to our "castle," or investments in the arts are enjoyable, helpful, and important parts of what we do, but they are not our foundation. Our foundation is Christ, a divinity made flesh, so that we might truly believe. His faith, his teaching, his healing, and his example are meant to show us that our God endures forever.

Extra Credit: Edward Mote (1797–1874) wrote the beloved hymn "My Hope Is Built." Growing up the child of poor innkeepers, Mote once commented that he thought Sundays were meant for playing in the streets of London.

As an adult, he became a Christian, serving God as a Baptist preacher and a hymn writer.

A *Word with the* "*Principal*": Eternal God, "on Christ the solid rock I stand; all other ground is sinking sand." Amen.

51. Red Sky

Object: *Weather Station*

Theme: *Contemplating the Mystery and Power of Creation*

Textbook Reading: *Genesis 1:7-8a ~ So God made the dome and separated the waters that were under the dome from the waters that were above the dome. And it was so. God called the dome Sky.*

Lesson: Until recently, a weather station for a classroom or school consisted of a thermometer, a windsock, and gauges for the barometric pressure, humidity, and rain. Kids checked the measurements, recorded the data, and gave their brief reports with a passive interest—unless the skies were threatening.

Now, schools are becoming equipped with more sophisticated technologies and are often linked to television weather centers that share information. Today's students take a more active interest in meteorology, boosted by a live broadcast from the eye of a hurricane, a movie romanticizing the work of tornado trackers, and the best-selling book *The Perfect Storm,* which portrays a storm system in all its fascination.

Despite our familiarity with the ancient signs and our knowledge from modern science, the weather still has its mysteries. And even in our nicely sheltered, climate-controlled lives, we are subject to the power of the weather, a power created by God.

Pop Quiz: What is the worst storm you have ever experienced?

A Word with the "Principal": God of the Sky, the more we learn, the more we are in awe of the mysteries and powers of your creation. Amen.

52. Gum Day

Object: *Chewing Gum*

Theme: *Following and Bending the Rules*

Textbook Reading: ***Psalm 19:7-8 ~ The law of the LORD is perfect, reviving the soul; the decrees of the LORD are sure, making wise the simple; the precepts of the LORD are right, rejoicing the heart; the commandment of the LORD is clear, enlightening the eyes.***

Lesson: Chewing gum? A classroom object? NO! NO! NO!

Most teachers, especially in elementary and middle schools, say no to chewing gum—with good reason, of course. Gum is distracting and, when not disposed of properly, can be messy and destructive. Chewing gum is against their rules.

One teacher has this to say about chewing gum in his fifth grade classroom:

> We have a hard and fast rule against the chewing of gum in my classroom; but towards the end of the year, we have Gum Day. For that day and that day only, my kids are allowed to chew gum. We've even studied the history of gum chewing, investigated where gum comes from and how it is refined, held a gum swap, played a gum relay game, and created sculpture from chewed chewing gum (it's true). And throughout the day, we talk about gum manners (no smacking or chewing while talking) and the proper disposal of gum.

This teacher holds Gum Day as a way of rewarding his students for obeying the rules. He also uses the occasion to discuss the bending and the keeping of rules. A reasonable teacher is willing to thoughtfully and creatively bend the rules when the time is right.

Extra Credit: Think about one of your classroom rules that could be creatively bent—just once!

A Word with the "Principal: O God, the setting and keeping of rules is such hard work; I pray for wisdom and insight. Amen.